GOD'S POEMS FOR YOU AND ME AS WE FACE GRIEF AND ADVERSITY

Inspired by God

Written by His servant, Nina Dean
who wrote these poems from God for all to see so that
they can be comforted as they comforted me

ISBN 979-8-89130-194-8 (paperback)
ISBN 979-8-89130-195-5 (digital)

Copyright © 2024 by Nina Dean

All rights reserved. No part of this publication may be reproduced, distributed, or transmitted in any form or by any means, including photocopying, recording, or other electronic or mechanical methods without the prior written permission of the publisher. For permission requests, solicit the publisher via the address below.

Christian Faith Publishing
832 Park Avenue
Meadville, PA 16335
www.christianfaithpublishing.com

Printed in the United States of America

Foreword

Inspired by her love for her husband and her Lord, this book is a love story written in poetic verse.

Nina is my dear friend whom I have known for over fifty years. We met at Goss Memorial Methodist Church. I have witnessed Nina grow in her faith and trust in our Lord through the years. Lately I notice her love for her Savior is growing exponentially. Nina is my prayer partner, and she is definitely a prayer warrior. She also has a lovely voice and sings in her church choir, and at any opportunity she has, she will sing.

After Jesse went to his eternal home, God began giving Nina poems. She awakens in the early hours with words that recall her memories with her Jesse, and the words rhyme. Jesse and Nina had a deep, enduring love for each other. Early in their marriage, Jesse took care of his child bride, as he called her. Later in their lives together, Nina took care of her dear Jesse. Nina is looking forward to meeting her Lord face-to-face and then turning to hug her sweet Jesse.

Jackie Eggerton

November 26, 2022, 9:00 a.m.

Thoughts of Me and You

As I lie here in our bed
Thoughts of you come into my head

Thoughts of me and you
And the things we used to do

We would take walks in the park, just me and you
Until you didn't know me, and I didn't know you

You would try to flee from the way things used to be
The way it used to be between you and me

Now there is just me without you, and I don't know what to do
You've lost the love from me, and I've lost the love from you

The tears start to fall because you are not with me and I am not with you
There is only me, and I don't know what to do

Grief comes to our door
Because there is no me and you anymore

It's not complete in our home where we used to be
Now there is no you, there is only me

But one day, we will be together just you and me
I will love you, and you will love me

And we will be together
With Jesus for all eternity.

November 26, 2022, at 4:59 p.m.

My Hatbox Full of Tears

I have a hatbox full of love letters that I have kept for forty-five years
Those letters showed your love for me. There were 153

The years have passed. You are ninety-five, and I am eighty-three
But I still remember your love and how you took care of me

I never thought about that hatbox over all these years
Now you are with Jesus, and all that remains is tears

That hatbox is full of tears and memories of the love you once had
     for me
You said I wrote eighty-four. Now I wish I had written you more

My life without you is not the same
My love for you will always remain

I will take that hatbox out now and then
To show my love for you once again.

The house is empty without you, dear
But I will always have the memories of when you were near

November 27, 2022

Notes about Me and You
Today, Yesterday, and Tomorrow

I thank God every day for today, yesterday, and tomorrow
As I now sit here alone in my sorrow

My life has changed from the way things used to be
Where there used to be two, there is now only me

My new life has now begun
Where there used to be two, now there is one

We had a life full of laughter and joy and sometimes tears
As we lived together for forty-five years

I spend my days alone in quiet solitude
Always and only thinking of you

The tomorrows will continue to come
But where there used to be two, there will always be one

You were my strength, my life, my reason for living
Where I spent my life with you, not taking but giving

You are no longer with me
The way our life used to be

Where there used to be two
Now there is only me

I don't know how many tomorrows God will give me
But I do know the day will come when we will live as one

There will be you and me the way it used to be
Where we will once again be together for all eternity

November 28, 2022

God Comes Shining Through

When we are alone, and we don't know what to do
God comes shining through

In our hour of need, and we don't know what to do
God comes shining through

If we need answers to our prayers, and we don't know what to do
God comes shining through.

He brings angels into our lives, who are our neighbors and friends
They go straight to work and bring our troubles to an end.

He reaches out to me, and he reaches out to you because He knows
    what to do
God comes shining through

There isn't anything that God can't do, if we just trust in Him, He
    will see us through
God comes shining through

So don't worry or fret,
He's not finished with you yet

He knows what to do.
God comes shining through

November 28, 2022

Jesus Carries Our Sorrows

Jesus carries our sorrows
When we have to face all our tomorrows

The tomorrows will come with waves of grief and tears
But I know my Jesus will be with me in all the coming years

When those waves of grief reach the shore of my life
My God will be with me to carry me through all that strife

He will carry my sorrows and wash away my tears
And He will be there to help me face my fears

Little by little, Jesus will drive those waves of grief away
So I will have the strength to face another day

Those waves of grief that we face every day will continue to come to
    the shore
Until that long-awaited day when Jesse, and I will once again become
    one forevermore.

November 29, 2022

Off with the Old, on with the New

Off with the old, on with the new
That's what God has in store for me and you

While we are still old and not new
God will be with us to see us through

He will one day take your hand or mine
And lead us to that heavenly place sublime

To a place of love
In heaven above

Now God has chosen that day to take you far away
And leave me behind to face another day

So I continue to wait here every day
For that time when He will take me away

To once again be with you
To be off with the old and on with the new

December 3, 2022, 7:59 a.m.

What Has Jesus Got in Store for Me Today

What does Jesus have in store for me today
When I have to face yet another day

Whatever problems arise in my home
I know I won't have to face them all alone

So when problems come knocking at my door
I know I won't have to face them alone anymore

Jesus will be at my side
To face problems that arise

He will be with me every step of the way
To help me get through yet another day

He will carry my sorrows
Through all my tomorrows

He's my strength and my guide
He will never leave my side

I have the faith to know
That He loves me so

So when another day comes, and grief is at my door
I know that Jesus will be with me forevermore

Until that day when He comes to take me
To be with Him for all eternity

December 4, 2022, at 10:30 a.m.

All Alone Sitting in This Church Pew

The hardest thing today for me to do
Is sit here alone in this church pew without you

You are sorely missed
At a time like this

I'm all alone sitting in this church pew
Because there is only me without you

You used to sit next to me in this church pew
But now there is only me without you

We would hold hands as we would always do
But now there is only me without you

Tears start to fall because you are not here with me
And it will never be the way it used to be

Once again, I will sit in this church pew
But there will only be me without you

I will always remember me sitting next to you
Holding hands and singing hymns like we used to do

It is very hard for me to sit in this pew today
As you are not with me. You are so far away

But on that final day God takes me away, we will be holding hands
    as we used to do
Singing praises in heaven where you will be with me and I will be
    with you

December 4, 2022, 10:30 a.m.

Have Unexpected Things Come into Your Life Today

As I sat in church today and heard the pastor say
"Have unexpected things come into your life today?"

I immediately thought how unexpected it was for me
For my sweet husband to pass so quickly

Then he said, "How many of you have lost husbands today?"
I raised my hand. Is he talking to me? My sweet husband just passed
     away

Then I thought to myself, when husbands pass, they are not lost but
     they are found
For they are now in heaven on holy ground

Jesus has taken them to their new home
Where they are surrounded by love and they are not lost and not
     alone

So when unexpected things come our way
God's peace will lead the way to help us face another day

God's billows of peace and love
Will come down from above

So I wait for that day when Jesus will take me away where I will not
     be lost, but I will be found
And I will join my sweet husband on holy ground

December 5, 2022, 10:30 a.m.

Every Time I Come Home

Every time I come home and open the door, you are not waiting
there for me anymore

It's not the way it used to be
Where you would be waiting there to greet me

If I stay home, I'm all alone
If I leave and come home, I'm still alone

So now you see how my life has changed
And how my life has been rearranged

But one day, God will open heaven's door
Where you will be there waiting to greet me once more

December 5, 2022, at 10:59 a.m.

You Have to Deal with Your Loss in Your Own Way

You have to deal with your loss in your own way
But God will be there to guide your steps every day

If you let Him in
He will turn your tears into a grin

He will always be there
Because He loves you and He cares

There is nothing He can't do
To help us and get us through

So don't feel that when you are there in your home
That you are sitting there all alone

He is always close by
To dry your tears when you cry

He will always bring you through your grief
At just the right time when you need that relief

So always put God before you in whatever you do
And He will put you on the right path and guide you through

So tomorrow when grief comes in the door
He will be there to carry your sorrow when you think you can't take
    it anymore

December 5, 2022, at 9:25 p.m.

God Gave Us Forty-Five Wonderful Years

God gave us forty-five wonderful, joy-filled years
Until dementia turned our joy into tears

When dementia came on to the scene
My sweet husband turned angry and mean

He didn't know what he was doin'
When he turned our life and home into ruin

Dementia brought profanity
Which hurt my Spirit of sanctity

But in some ways, my sweet husband knew
Of the things he was putting me through

He would apologize to me
And wished our life was the way it used to be

God gave my husband ninety-five wonderful years
Now all that is left are memories and tears

He used to be able to see, hear, laugh, and sing
And he used to do wonderful things

Now because all of that was taken away
My sweet husband would often say: "Why doesn't God take me today?"

But now I can rejoice
He is in heaven singing in his new voice

He is now waiting for me
Where we can once again live and sing in harmony

December 6, 2022, at 9:00 a.m.

What's Keeping Me Up at Night

What is keeping me up at night
Memories of you when you would hold me tight

Memories of things we used to do
When I was me, and you were you

When I would love you, and you would love me
And our life would be back to the way it used to be

We would sit side by side
And you would call me your child bride

You would look at me and compliment me
When you used to be you, and I used to be me

Now when I come into the room, it's empty
Where you used to be, there is only me

I miss you not being there in your chair
The room is empty, and you're not there

Once again, the tears begin to fall
Because you were my all and all

But there will come a time when we will be we
You will be you, and I will be me together for all eternity

December 6, 2022, 11:00 a.m.

God's Love Comes Pouring Out of Me

God's love comes pouring out of me
In the form of words of love in poetry

He is bringing back memories
When I loved you, and you loved me

Memories that still warm my heart
Even though we are now so far apart

We would laugh, and we would cry
But God has always been there for you and I

We would pray and then
We would ask God to make things right again

God's love is still surrounding you and me
As I wait to join you for all eternity

December 6, 2022, 9:52 p.m.

Words Every Waking Minute of the Day

Words every waking minute of the day
God keeps pouring out words to me and what to say

Words when I have to quickly grab a pen and write what I receive
For as quickly as the words would come, they would leave

Words of memories that will never end
When you were my husband and my friend

Words about my friends and family
And how they have been reaching out to me

Words that they know I am home sitting all alone
As I sit there waiting for the ring of the phone

Words as I sit here remembering how things were when you were
    here with me
But now I know things will never, never be like they used to be

Words that I have to start a new life for me without you
But I know that God will once again carry me through

Words that I also know there will come a day
When God will choose the time and date to take me away

Words on that day when there will be a Celebration of Life for me
As I celebrate that day when I will be in heaven with you for all
    eternity

Words that you can read once again
About my life with my husband, who was also my friend

Words that I will tuck away, and there they will be
When you can read them as part of my eulogy

December 8, 2022, 3:29 p.m.

Where Once We Will Become Me and You

I sleep a good bit of the day
Because you are so far away

I think of things we used to do
When I was me, and you were you

Now I only have memories
When you were you, and I was me

There are times when I'm happy and times when I'm sad
When I stop to think of the things that we had

Tears coming streaming down my cheek
Every now and then throughout the week

I'm wishing you were here so we could talk
Or maybe just go for a walk

There is nothing more that I can do
But just sit here and think about you

As I sit here writing this poem, I'm so lonely
I wish there was something I could do to bring you back to me

Hours go by, and I wish I had just a glimpse of you
So we could talk and laugh the way we used to do

But that will never be the way it used to be
When you were you, and I was me living together so happily

I must find a way to end this poem
As I sit here so all alone

So all I can say is there will come a day
When God will come to take me away

Where once again I can be with you
And we can become me and you

December 9, 2022, 1:03 a.m.

Poems from God for Me and You

The days keep slipping by as they always do
And I continue to write poems while I'm thinking about you

These poems are about you
And the love we once knew

Poems that comfort me and fill my heart
Although we are still so far apart

My days and nights are full of tears
Just thinking about you and all those years

I must build a new life without you, my dear
But I have no fear because I know God is always near

But what God is doing for me most of all
He is filling my days with friends and family who call
They are concerned for me because I am all alone

So they continue to call me and pray for me on the telephone

Before I know it, the hours have gone by
As I continue to think about you and I

Evening draws near and once again you are not here
And our home is so empty without you, my dear

The hardest part for me is at the end of the day
When you are still so far away

Never to see the face I once knew
When you loved me, and I loved you

So once again I must sleep alone
Until one day God will call me home

And when that day comes, we will be together you and me
Where we will spend our lives together for all eternity

December 9, 2022, 8:00 a.m.

Where There Is Me and Where There Is You

Where there is me and where there is you
That's where I want to be the whole day through

But I know that can never be
You can only exist in the heart of me

Only in my thoughts of you and me
Can that be a reality

So when I am sleeping and dreaming of you
That's when I can spend my time with you

And in that place
I can see your face

I can hug you, and you can hug me
But when I wake up, there is no you, there is only me

Then reality comes knocking at my door
For there is no you and me anymore

So then I must wait until evening comes
Where once again in my dreams we can become one

God woke me up with this poem for you
As he consistently continues to do

One day my dream will become a reality
When I'm with you, and you're with me for all eternity

This is the way all my poems must end
When I can be with my husband, who is also my friend

December 9, 2022, 9:21 a.m.

When I See the Sun Shine

Each day when I wake up and I see the sunshine
I can't get you out of my mind

So once again I must face each new day
Knowing that you are so far away

But God's light continues to shine
On this new life of mine

God is opening new doors that I must go through
While I live my new life without you

It's not easy you see
As we used to go through those doors when you were with me

But God is always there shining through
As I face my new life without you

So it will always remain
The days will be the same

Those days will turn into years
When there will always be tears

My comfort is knowing even though we will be apart
You will always, always be still in my heart

December 12, 2022, 7:20 a.m.

God Wants to Keep in Touch with You

God wants to keep in touch with you
For He knows what you are going through

He wakes you in your morning hour
Because He has all the power

He wants to be there
To meet your every care

He knows you have sleepless nights because of what's ahead of you
But once again, God knows what to do

We must lean on the Holy Spirit for His power
And not worry or fret every waking hour

Once again, I know God will go before me
To take care of my every need

But again, the flesh makes us worry and fret
When God says, "I'm not finished with you yet"

He has plans for me that I'm not even aware of
As He continues to meet my every need and show His love

I go on with my day
Knowing He is not far away

So when you are discouraged and don't know what to do
God will keep in touch and take care of you

December 12, 2022, 8:00 a.m.

God Is Opening New Doors in My Life

It's incredible how God is opening new doors
To help me with my problems and more

When I don't know what to do
I know God will carry me through

He goes before me every day
To show me what path to take along the way

He is opening new doors every day
To send more new friends my way

By bringing new friends into my life
To spend time with me as I go through this strife

They meet me in church and sit with me
Because they know things are not the way they used to be

They send me emails, call me on the telephone
Or send a note to comfort me while I'm all alone

I am meeting old friends that I haven't seen in years
And they give me a big hug and dry away my tears

Just when I think my new life is not the way it used to be
God sends old and new friends into my life to comfort me

So when you think your old life has come to an end
He will send old and new friends into your life to start again.

December 12, 2022, 11:34 a.m.

I'm a Widow but I'm Not Alone as God Meets My Needs by Telephone

I am a widow, but I'm not all alone
God is helping me while I sit at home

He answers my prayers while I'm at home
As I sit here and wait for the ring of the telephone

I put a prayer request in church on Sunday about my insecurity about
    my Social Security
Although by faith I know that God will answer my prayers and meet
    my needs

So now it is Monday, and I sit here waiting by the phone
Trying to solve my problems, but I'm not alone

God took care of all my problems for me
And He even took care of my Social Security

So if problems come knocking at your door
God is there to meet your problems and more

You only have to have faith and believe
And God will answer and you will receive

December 14, 2022, 5:00 p.m.

The Hours Go By and the Day Goes By

The hours go by, and the day goes by
I wake up from my nap, and there is still no you, only I

I sit here alone praying you could be here with me the way it used
 to be
And I would wake up, and I would hug you and you would hug me

I know sweetheart there is a reason why you cannot be here with me
For God's angels have taken you to your eternal home for all eternity

While I am missing you, and you are missing me, the sweet God
 above
Is filling you and me with His unending love

Though we remain miles apart
You are still here in my heart

The day turns into night
But God is taking care of me, and I'm alright

You used to be by my side and took care of me so lovingly
Now Jesus has taken your place, and now you see He is taking care
 of me

God planned our life many years ago. He said He would never leave
 and forsake you and me
So He will be here with me until I can be there with you for all
 eternity

December 14, 2022, 6:05 p.m.

Another Day Has Come to an End

Another day has come to an end
It is time for me to drive to the mailbox again

It brings back another memory
When you used to ride to the mailbox with me

It was just another way to give you something to do
Where we could spend time together just me and you

It is now time for me to check the mailbox and see
If there are any cards and letters, and hopefully, no bills waiting there
      for me

I receive comforting cards and letters of sympathy
As old and new friends reach out to me

So you see, my sweet Jesse, even though you are so far away
God finds ways to take care of me every day

I still continue to miss you, my sweet Jesse
Until we can be together just you and me

I will wait for that day God takes me to be with you
When we can be together to do the things we used to do

December 20, 2022, 10:51 p.m.

How Do I Spend Christmas without You

Christmas is coming. Now what do I do
How do I spend Christmas without you

All I do is think about you
And all the wonderful things that we used to do

We would drive out into the night
And look at all the Christmas lights

Once there was fun and laughter in our home
Now it is so silent, and I'm all alone

We would spend time with family
Now all I can think of is the way things used to be

Now there is no visiting family
There isn't you. There is only me

No reading cards together from friends and family
That would always bring back that special memory

There is no gift or beautiful card from you
What do I have to look forward to

There will be no gift or beautiful card from me
There will be no gifts under the tree

It will be almost more than I can take
On that lonely Christmas morning when I awake

When God reminds me that Christmas is not always about gifts and
    cards and family
It is about the birth of the Christ child, who was born for you and me

So now I know that I will never be alone
Jesus is always right beside me in our home

Jesus will help me face Christmas and the coming days without you
    when I don't know what to do
Until Jesus chooses that special day when you will always be with me,
    and I will always be with you

December 22, 2022, 9:13 a.m.

I Wake Up, My Dear, and You're Not Here with Me

I wake up, my dear, and you're not here with me
I look over at your pillow where you are supposed to be

I begin another day without you
And I'm still trying to learn what to do

We spent our days together, you and I
So now I must begin another day without you, and I cry

I must accept the fact
That you are not coming back

But that is not easy to do
As I face each day without you

We talked about the times God would take you or me away
I guess I just didn't think I would have to face that day, and it would
     be this way

I never ever knew
What it would be like to face life without you

It is not easy being left behind
You are constantly on my mind

But each and every day
God is helping me find my way

And He is always here
To wipe away my every tear

God is teaching me each day how to start a new life
But I will always love you, and I will always be your wife

So again, the tears start to fall
Because you were my all and all

I am waiting for the day we will meet face to face
And I will join you in that heavenly place

December 22, 2022, 11:21 a.m.

Almost Every Day My Life Begins
and Ends with a Poem

Almost every day my life begins and ends with God's poem
Because I must face a new life where it is silent and quiet, and I'm
    all alone

So why do I sit here all alone as God helps me write yet another poem
The reason is because God has taken my sweet dear husband to His
    new home

So I sit here and think, *What do people do without God in their heart*
When they have to face that day when their beloved will depart

God will wake you up and give you strength for that day
And He will always let you know that He is not far away

So make it a priority to spend time with God each day
And He will guide you and show you every step of the way

He sends His angels to guide you through every step that you take
They never sleep. They are always awake

So when you get to that point when you don't know what to do
Spend time with God, and He will carry you through

He will lighten your load and carry your sorrows
As you face all your tomorrows

December 24, 2022, 6:28 a.m.

Our Little Angel Christmas Tree

It is Christmas Eve, and I wake up with thoughts of you and me
As I sit here alone by our little angel Christmas tree

I look at this tree that has been up all these years
And all of a sudden, my face is wet with tears

As I remember the first year we put up our little angel Christmas tree
And placed it on that table where it now stands as it always will be

I have memories of that first Christmas when we had gifts under the
tree
From me to you and you to me and gifts from friends and family

So when Christmas was over, and it was time to take the tree down,
You said, "No, why don't we just leave it up all year round"

This year there are no gifts from me to you and you to me under our
little angel Christmas tree
God has taken you to where you wanted to be, and all that's left are
tears and memories

When Christmas comes again, I will be thinking of you and me
As I sit by our little angel Christmas tree

This poem now ends with thoughts of you and me and when we will
receive
That special gift from God that we will be together again for all
eternity

December 26, 2022, 5:31 a.m.

What Do I Do at the End of 2022

What do I do at the end of 2022
When I have to face a New Year without you
A new year without you by my side

But I know God will be my guide

There will be no new pictures of me and you at the end of 2022
Because you won't be here with me to celebrate it with you

So as I face the new year of 2023
There will be no you, there will only be me

I will not have you by my side
But I know in my heart God will provide

It won't be the same without you, my dear
As once again I feel another tear

But I know God has a plan for you and me
His plan is for you and me to be together with Him for all eternity.

December 26, 2022, 3:24 p.m.

I Finished Another Poem from God Today

Hi, honey, I finished another poem from God today.
I wonder how many more are on the way

He gives me one or two almost every day
Because they are all about you while you are away

He knows about you as he sees you every day
So I guess this is his way of letting me know that you are okay

The words fill my Spirit and our home
While I sit here without you all alone

So this is the way I spend my day
Thinking of you when you are so far away

I read them to friends who feel the same way
As their husband or wife has passed away

It comforts us to know that you and they are not alone
As God has taken you and them to their new home

I wish you could be beside me as I write this poem
This gift that God has given me when I sit here all alone

It comforts me as I write this poem
Because one day, I will be with you in our heavenly home

December 27, 2022, 8:11 p.m.

Sweetheart, You Are Still Not Here with Me

Sweetheart, you are still not here with me
You're up there with Jesus where you should be

Boots (our family cat) and I took a nap today
But you are still so far away

I wake up, and you are still not here
I want to reach out and give you a hug, my dear

I miss you more and more every day
And you are still so far away

Though we are miles and miles apart
You are still here with me in my heart

The day lingers on and turns into night
And God is still taking care of me, and I'm alright

I used to take care of you, and you used to take care of me so lovingly
But Jesus has taken your place, and He is right beside me

So no matter how God makes this poem rhyme for you and me
He will make sure that we will always end up together for all eternity

December 27, 2022, 8:47 p.m.

It Is the Evening of December 27, 2022, and the Time Is 8:47

It is the evening of December 27, 2022, and the time is eight
    forty-seven
And I know, my sweet Jesse, that you are with Jesus in heaven

The hours go by
And I continue to cry

I know one day the tears will be gone
But right now, the tears linger on

I continue to think of you and the life we once knew
When you knew me, and I knew you

The times we traveled and sang in quartets
The fun we had and the friends we met

The days go by, and I continue to cry
When I think of sweet memories of you and I

It is so lonely here in our home without you
It's not fair you left me and didn't take me with you

So I'm waiting for that special day
When God will take me away

To spend forever with God alone
In our new eternal home

December 29, 2022, 11:23 p.m.

Jesse, It's Getting Close to New Year's Eve, and You Are Not Here with Me

Jesse, it's getting close to New Year's Eve, and you are not here with
    me
You left me to be with Jesus where you wanted to be for all eternity

So now I'm left here in our home
And I sit here all alone

I must face the New Year of 2023
And I'm not sure what God has in store for me

God gave us forty-five years together on our wedding anniversary of
    October 7
And then on the day of October 19 at seven ten, He took you to
    heaven

We often talked about how it would be
Would I go before you, or would you go before me

Since I was eighty-three and you were ninety-five
You often called me your child bride

In the last couple of years of those forty-five
Some drastic changes came into our lives

Because in 2021, dementia came walking in the door
And you, my sweet loving husband, were not there anymore

You turned into a man I never knew
And I didn't know what to do

You had no control over what you would say or do
Because that is the way dementia changed you

At times you would say to me (because I think you knew), "I'm so
        sorry for what I am putting you through."
I would say to you, "That's okay, honey, we'll get through this
        together, and God will show us what to do."

All those years you had taken care of me, so now it was time for me
        to take care of you
It's been a long journey, my sweet husband, but God was there to
        bring you and me through

Once again, God has told me what I should do.
I must make this final decision to let God take care of you

Now just as this poem began, you are in your new body, and you are
        a new man
And God is taking care of you as only He can

I will wait here while God continues to take care of me
Until that time when we can be together for all eternity

December 31, 2022

Foreword to God's Book of Poems

Jesse and I celebrated forty-five years of marriage on October 7, 2022
We didn't exchange gifts and cards like we used to do

Actually, it was not a celebration,
It was merely an observation

An observation of all those happy years we spent together as husband
and wife
But in the last two years of those forty-five, there was a dramatic
change in our life

Dementia had taken over Jesse's life
And we battled it together as husband and wife

Now this battle with dementia has come to an end
As my sweet Jesse passed in hospice on October 19, 2022, at 7:10
p.m.

His "Celebration of Life" service was on November 19, 2022, at 2:00
p.m.
And my life was never the same again

On November 26, 2022, God began to speak to me in the quiet and
peace of our home
As he showed me how to create a poem

God would wake me up with just a few words in the early morn
And all of a sudden a poem was born

Since that very first morning, God has spoken to me
In the quiet of our home about my sweet Jesse

Poems have begun pouring out of me
Of memories of my sweet Jesse and how our life used to be

God has brought old and new friends back into my life
Now I am a widow, but in my heart, I'm still Jesse's wife

God keeps giving me poems day by day
As my sweet Jesse is so far away

God continues to help me write many, many poems
And He wants those poems to find a home

In my thoughts and prayers, God has spoken to me,
"Why don't you put those poems in a book for all to see"

So as you read this book of poems God has given to me
Let them comfort you as they have comforted me

And perhaps when you do God will speak to you

And on another early morn
A poem will be born

Wednesday, January 4, 2023, 5:31 p.m.

Here It Is January 4, 2023, and Jesse, You Are Not Here with Me

Here it is January 4, 2023
And, Jesse, you are not here with me

I must face this New Year without you, my dear
With only memories of when you were here

At that time, I didn't want to leave our home
And leave you sitting there all alone

I am going to do what I couldn't do before
While I was taking care of you and more

God said I must learn to fill my days
While you are still so far away

So, Jesse, I want you to know that once again
I am playing dominoes with our friends

I am also going to join the choir and sing God's love
As you look down on me with love from above

Tonight, I went to a Bible study
Hosted by Keith and Molly

They had the Bible study upstairs
So I had to ascend and descend the stairs with care

You were in my thoughts while I was at the Bible study
Wishing you could have been there with me

I met some old and new friends at this Bible study
There was room for you to sit right beside me

The Bible study started at seven and ended at nine
I had to descend the stairs at quite a steep incline

There were refreshments at the end of the Bible study
But I just wanted to get on the road and get home safely

So I thanked our hosts, Keith and Molly
For inviting me to their Bible study

The angels were with me on the road leaving Keith and Molly's
As they protected and escorted me back to our home safely

So my new life will go on without you, my sweet Jesse
Until we can be together with Jesus for all eternity

January 5, 2023, 7:30 a.m.

I Woke Up This Early Morn, and Another Poem Was Born

I woke up this early morn
And another poem was born

God puts words in my head
As I lay awake in our bed

This old song came into my mind
As you, dear Jesse, left me here behind

This old Irving Berlin tune
Filled my thoughts and our bedroom

"You keep coming back like a song"
And then I added because you are not here where you belong

The song goes on to say, "Can't run away from you, dear
I've tried so hard, but I fear You'll always follow me near and far"

Just when I think that I'm set,
Just when I've learned to forget I close my eyes, dear, and there you are

This old Irving Berlin tune continues to fill the room as I go on to say
It brings memories of you and me as you are so far away

And here is the tune
That continues to fill our bedroom

You keep coming back like a song
A song that keeps saying remember

The sweet used to be that was once you and me
Keeps coming back like an old melody

The perfume of roses in May
Return to my room in December

From out of the past where forgotten things belong
You keep coming back like a song

Dear Jesse, when we were apart
Your love letters filled my heart

I realized, Jesse, this song is about you and me and the way things
     used to be
And as this old Berlin tune says, "You keep coming back to me like
     an old melody"

You do keep coming back like a song
Because in my memories this is where you belong

But once again, Jesse, God ends this poem about you and me
And God promises me that we will be together for all eternity

January 6, 2023, 6:01 a.m.

God Woke Me Up at 6:01 and Another Poem from God Has Begun

God woke me up at 6:01
And another poem from God has begun

So start your day and make a new way
And listen to what God has to say

God and I have been communicating day by day
Since my dear Jesse passed away

He has given me these precious words to share
Because He is in my life, and He cares

He is always here with me
And His words meet my every need

Why did God choose me to speak to every day
Because I take the time to listen to what he has to say

His words keep pouring out of me more and more
As waves continue to come in and touch the shore

God's words are true
They belong to me and you

God loves you, and He cares
And He is just waiting to share

He wants to talk to you and meet with you
He wants to be there to show you what to do

When sorrows come your way every day
He can carry those sorrows and make the sadness go away

So take a pad and pencil in your hand and sit in your chair
And wait for God to talk to you and listen to what He wants to share

In the silence of the day
He will take those cares away

He did it for me, He will do it for you
So take that time and let God comfort you

January 12, 2023, 3:09 a.m.

I Am Giving You a Holy Life

God woke me up with these words, "I am giving you a holy life
As you remain in your home as Jesse's wife"

Jesse, I didn't know this would happen so quickly
As God took you to your heavenly home before me

I'm sitting here writing these words from God
As you are waiting for me on holy sod

Our lives have drastically changed
And oh, my sweet Jesse, how your life has been rearranged

Words, words from God every day
As I think of you, my sweet Jesse, as I pray

I will speak out God's word every day
I can do all things through Christ who strengthens me and I add
     come what may

God gave me this poem at three nine. It is now four nine
As God continues to make these words rhyme

It's not the end. It is just the beginning
As I wait here for God in my first inning

So I will wait to join you, my sweet Jesse
Until we can be together for all eternity

January 16, 2023, 1:23 a.m.

Jesus Is Helping Me Build and Start a New Life

Jesus is helping me build and start a new life
As I sit here left behind as my sweet dear husband, Jesse's, wife

He is helping me get through each and every day
And giving me words to share and say while you, my sweet Jesse, are
    so far away

I didn't know this would happen to me
As God took you before me, my sweet Jesse

Once again God wakes me up with these words to share
Because He loves me, and He wants to comfort me and let me know
    He cares

So I am sitting here writing these words from God
While you are waiting for me on holy sod

Our lives have recently changed
And your life, my sweet Jesse, has been rearranged

It's not the end. It is just the beginning
As I wait here left behind to start my first inning

I'm waiting to join you in your new home up there
As I wait here in our home under Jesus's care

So I know God has a special place picked out for me
And that place is for you and me to spend our life together for all
    eternity

January 17, 2023

God Woke Me Up in the Morning Light

Jesse, God woke me up in the morning light
And gave me His words to write

God says He knows what I am going through
So He will give me things to do

He fills my day with friends old and new
And they fill my day with things we can do

He wants me to continue my life without you
Until that day when one will become two

He continues to give me thoughts, my dear Jesse, of me and you
And all those wonderful years we were together and the things we
    used to do

He says the tears will continue to come
Until that day He will make us one

So my life will go on and on until that final day
That God will take me away

And then once again we will be you and me
And we will be together for all eternity

January 21, 2023, 11:09 a.m.

God Has Been Making Changes in My Life

Good morning, my sweet Jesse, since you passed on October 19,
    2022, to be with God for all eternity
God has been speaking to me and giving me words in poems to write
    about you and me

So I wanted to share with you as your wife
About the changes that God has been making in my life

He gave me a gift I never knew I had
He gave me words in a poem about our life, the happy and the sad

He speaks to me morning, noon, and night
And gives me the words that I must write

When I receive these words, and God tells me what to do
Another poem is born about how I am waiting here to be with you

I never thought that God would use me in this way
While He took you, my sweet husband, so far away

Jesse, did you ever think that you were married to a poet
And you didn't even know it

It was certainly a surprise to me as it is probably a surprise to you
That God would use poems to communicate with me, and I com-
    municate with you

When He speaks to me, I listen to every word He has to say
Then God helps me write another poem in a new and creative way

Hmm, Jesse, I got to thinking, since God Almighty created you and me
And the world above and the world below and everything we see

Why wouldn't our God above
Take the time to show his love

And create poems about you and me
For all the world to see

Jesse, I think this is God's way to comfort me while I remain here
        without you
Because at times, I wish you were here with me, or I was there with you

So, my dear Jesse, I will be here every day
To share God's gift and pray

I will continue to write His poetry for all the world to see
Until that final day, He will take me to be with you for all eternity

February 4, 2023, 3:00 a.m.

Thoughts God Gave to a Widow in a Rhyme as This Widow Is Left Behind

Jesse, once again I woke up at 3:00 a.m. thinking about you and me
    and what you left behind
And all these thoughts go spinning and spinning around in my mind

Boots, our sweet pet cat, who misses you as much as I do, whom you
    also left behind with me
Woke up and jumped on the back of the computer chair and is won-
    dering why I am up at three

The reason I woke up at three
Is because there is no you but only me

After reading my will, after you preceded me
I am left with all these responsibilities

These responsibilities used to be yours and now they are mine
And that is why these thoughts are spinning around in my mind

You took such good care of me and made all the right decisions
But now those decisions are mine and not yours and that's not what
    I envisioned

I must not only think of my children but your children too
When the time comes when God will take me to my new home to
    be with you

So once again, Jesse, I am faced with all these decisions to make
Not only for your children but for my children's sake

Everything must be equally divided between your children and mine
When God finally takes me and leaves them behind

I must think of our home and all the contents and our car
Who will be responsible for them when we are where we are

Jesse, it is a big responsibility that you left with me
I thank God that He will help me make the right decisions about
        how it should be

How do people live without God when all these decisions have to be
        made
Who will be responsible and finally come to their aid

Once again, God woke me up at three with thoughts of you and me
        and my responsibilities
I wrote down all the thoughts God gave to me as I certainly could not
        depend on my memory at eighty-three

God gave these thoughts to me in a poem
Until the time I can be with you in our new home

Who knows how many more poems God will put inside of me
        beyond February 4 in 2023
Until I can be with you, my sweet Jesse, for all eternity

February 11, 2023, 12:05 p.m.

Poems to Comfort Me and You
as We Face Our Life Anew

As I was taking my nap today
Jesus woke me up with these things to say

Jesus came into my future to show me the way to go
Because as I continue to reap, I will continue to sow

I have to leave my memories behind and start life anew
I have to learn to get involved with other things to do

It is not easy for me to face the past
When my sweet loved one has passed

The future is not the way I thought it would be
Because once there was me and you, and now there is only me

I thought we would be together in all the years to come
But now there is no we, there is only one

How do I fill each passing day
I must look to God to see what He has to say

So when it is quiet and peaceful in our home
I must listen to God, for He is here, and I am not alone

He speaks to me while I am asleep or awake
He shows me and tells me what path I must take

He said He created us to fellowship, and we should set aside time to
    spend with Him
So I continue to read His word and live for Him avoid mistakes and
    not sin

It's not easy for me, but then it was not easy for Him
When he died on the cross to forgive me for my sin

I ask myself again, "How do people get through this life"
Where there is no husband, there is only a wife

I have to lean on Jesus each and every day
And He will wipe away my tears and show me the way

He fills my days and nights with things to do
And He fills my life with friends, old and new

Jesus said He will show me that I can fill my days and nights in so
    many new ways
He said to join the choir, join a Bible study, and fill your nights and
    your days

When once again, you will face the day with nothing to do
He said I will bring old friends out of the past to comfort you

The phone will ring, and it will be a voice from the past
And I will have time to share about my life and my loved one, who
    has passed

Jesus will never leave us or forsake us because He loves us and knows
    what to do
That's how Jesus came into my life to guide me, and He will guide you

Jesus makes it so simple to follow Him
As he turns our tears into a grin

So once again, my dear friends
Listen as this poem ends

Jesus came into my life and has given me poems to write about me
    and you
And I pray as these poems comforted me, they will comfort you as
    we face our life anew

February 13, 2023, 5:00 p.m.

Thoughts of My Husband
Came to Me Today

This wonderful thought came to me today
While my dear sweet husband is so far away

Wouldn't it be nice if today God would release our husbands on loan
And let them come to visit us for a few days while we sit here alone

Every day, I have this constant ache inside of me
I just wish my sweet husband was near me the way it used to be

If God would do this for me today
I know it would take this constant ache away

We could visit and talk
We could hold hands and go for a walk

We could take a walk to the mailbox at the end of the day
And pray there would not be waiting there too many bills to pay

We could do the things we used to do
When we used to be me and you

I could tell him how much I love him, and he could tell me how
   much he loves me
We could once again have our meals together and enjoy each other's
   company

We could once again take communion and read God's word together
And thank him for today, yesterday, and forever

He could spend the night
And we could hold each other tight

I could look over at his pillow, and there he would be
Then I could lay my head on my pillow and sleep peacefully

We could wake up in the morning and talk about the weather
And then we could have our breakfast together

I know this could only happen in a dream
But wouldn't that be a wonderful scheme

Then we could accept all those lonely days when our husbands are
    so, so far away
Because then we could pray that God would let them come into our
    dreams to visit us another day

So at the end of the day, and I lay my head on the pillow, to my hus-
    band I say good night
I will pray that God will bring my sweet husband back into my
    dreams tonight

February 27, 2023, 11:02 a.m.

Sweet Jesse, You Are Always on My Mind

Sweet Jesse, you are always on my mind
I think about you all of the time

You went ahead of me and left me behind
And I think to myself, *That wasn't very kind*

I go to bed thinking of you
I wake up thinking of you

My life is not the same
And you're to blame

I know you are in heaven up there
And you are in God's loving care

It's just so hard to face life each day without you
All I want to do is sleep and dream of you

I wake up day after day, and nothing has changed
My life without you has been so rearranged

We can't eat breakfast together or lunch or supper too
How do I face each day after day, after day without you

Jesse, do you know what is happening in this world today
While you are up in heaven so far away?

Remember when we used to pray for revival in our devotions every day
Well, I am here to tell you today that revival is on the way

It started in a college in a prayer meeting in Kentucky
And now it has spread to a college in Tennessee

It is spreading to colleges all over the country and all the world to see
I just wish you could be here to experience it with me

I have to experience this new life without you
And without you beside me, it is hard to do

Because when my future comes into view
All I see is a life without you

I could go on and on with this poem
As I sit here this morning all alone

So all I can hope for is that day
When Jesus will take me far away

And I can see you, and you can see me
And once again, life will be the way it used to be

I will be with you, and you will be with me
And we can face our new life together for all eternity

March 1, 2023, 10:50 a.m.

Once Again, Dear Jesse, Another Poem about You Because I Am Missing You

Once again it is morning, and I wake up, my dear
I look over at your pillow, and you are not here

I begin another day without you
And I don't know what to do

I must face each day
When you are away

I must accept the fact
That you are not coming back

We talked about the times when God would take us away
I just didn't think it would be this way

But God was kind
He took you and left me behind

I guess I never knew
What it would be to face life without you

It is not easy being left behind
Because you are constantly on my mind

But each and every day
God is helping me and leading the way

He fills me with poems to write to you almost every day
It makes the minutes, the hours, and the days melt away

Once again
This poem must end

I will wait to be with you, and you will wait to be with me
And we will spend our time together for all eternity

March 10, 2023

Easter Has Passed, and There Is No We, There Is Only Me

Easter has passed, and there is no we
There is only me

It is now Monday, and the tears continue to fall
Because you were my all and all

I sang in the choir on Easter Sunday to celebrate Resurrection day
But again you were not with me as you were in heaven so far away

I looked over at that church pew where we used to sit, me and you
It brought tears to my eyes because there was only me, and there was
    no you sitting in the church pew

We sat your walker beside the church pew
Where we sat together as me and you

I saw couples sitting in the church pew ahead of me
It reminded me of me and you when we used to be we

It is still so lonely without you sitting beside me
Because there is no we, there is only me

The service is over, and I feel so lonely
Because there is no we, there is only me

The flowering Cross in front of the church was there
But no pictures of you and me were taken to share

I didn't want to take pictures at the cross
Because I was all alone, and I felt oh so lost

Because there was no we
There was only me

I was invited to have dinner with Frank and Ginny, who are friends
        in my church family
But once again there was no we, there was only me

I am still having problems putting the past away
As I wake up every morning to face another day

It is oh so quiet in our home
Where once again I must sit here all alone

What am I to do
As I sit here without you

You are not here
And there are only tears

Now it is Monday, and I must face another day
When I am without you, and you are still in heaven so far away

I think I am going to get out my hatbox full of tears
And reread those letters from you that I kept for forty-five years

The letters you wrote to me to show your love for me
When I loved you, and you loved me, and I can remember the way
        our life used to be

Those letters will be filled with all those memories
When I was me, and you were you, and we were we

I thank God that He gave me this poem today
To bring you closer to me in this special way

So once again I will end this poem about you and me
Until the day that we will be we for all eternity

March 13, 2023, 1:00 p.m.

Since My Dear Husband, Jesse, Passed Away

Since my dear husband, Jesse, passed away
God has been giving me poems almost every day

These poems are about my husband and I
As the minutes, the hours, and the days pass by

God showed me
How to write poetry

Every time I read a story
And friends talk to me

A poem that God gives to me
Comes pouring out of me

It is very quiet in my home
As I sit here all alone

And because of the quiet and peace—*Shalom*
God's words speak to me, and they turn into another poem

So why don't you take time to stop and listen to what God has to say
    to you
And perhaps God will help you to become a poet too

Now I will take this time to say to you today
I pray one of God's poems will come your way

March 14, 2023, 3:00 a.m.

How Many More Times Will God Wake Me Up at Night

How many more times will God wake me up at night
As He continues to give me these poems to write

He gives me lines
Two at a time

And these lines
Begin to rhyme

I just want to go to sleep
As I have an appointment to keep

The appointment is for a surprise birthday party for Jackie Eggerton,
    my dear friend
To celebrate her ninetieth birthday with all her friends

So I ask God will this night ever end
So I can make that appointment with Jackie, my dear prayer partner,
    and my friend

It started at 3:00 a.m. It is now 4:00 a.m.
As I continue to write words from God again and again

If I don't continue to write these words from God I receive
Those words will take flight and leave

This is my story to you today
As God has given me these words to say

I must write these words down, or they will go away
Or maybe they will return another day. Who's to say?

So now I tell Jesus I must go to sleep
As I have an appointment to keep

Tears Once Again Keep Falling Down

Tears once again keep falling down
As I sit here alone in our car driving all around

I have memories of you and me commenting on all the beautiful
    scenery
As I would drive to church with you sitting next to me

It's so hard to sit in the car without you
And think of all the wonderful things we used to do

I remember the time when you turned ninety
And you were driving, not me

We were on our way
To celebrate your ninetieth birthday

Your children rented a house for the weekend near Disney
Where we could all join together as one big happy family

I was seventy-eight, and I thought it was great
To gather with your family and mine to celebrate

This will always remain in my memory today
Of that wonderful weekend, we celebrated your ninetieth birthday

Now it was time to return to our home with you at the wheel and
    not me
As I sat next to you the way it used to be

As we returned home who knows how this could be
But we ended up in the back lots of Disney

We finally found our way to I-4
And we were not lost anymore

These are the memories that keep coming back to me
As I enjoyed our life with you, dear Jesse, the way it used to be

Now as always, this poem must come to an end
And I long for the day when I can be with you once again

One day that day will come
When we will become one

So it won't matter who is driving, you or me
We will once again be together commenting on heaven's scenery

March 18, 2023, 12:30

Another Poem Is Born

I woke up at four thirty in the early morn
And God's poems were born

He gave me three poems, one, two, three
And I went back to bed at nine thirty

I took the phone and my glasses with me
In case the phone would ring and wake me

It is now twelve thirty, and I am up again
As God's poems never end

I will go on with my day
And check the email and pray

I'm sure God has more poems on the way
So I will wait to see what God has to say

It is now time to feed our pet cat, Boots, again
Because he grieves with me, and he is my live-in friend

He sleeps with me at the foot of the bed
As on the pillow, I lay my head

Now I must take time to feed myself
As I put God's poem on the shelf

March 18, 2023, at 4:30 a.m.

Love Passes by for Jess and I

Love passes by
For Jess and I

It's in the past
But our love lasts

We had forty-five wonderful years
And now I'm left with all these tears

Scenes of the past are what I see
As we took walks in the park just you and me

I see all these places in the park
Where you remained there after dark

I see a bench where you used to go and sit to escape from me
Again this brings back more aches, tears, and memories

What am I going to do with all these memories
When I constantly think of you and me

Once again, this poem of line after line comes pouring out of me
As I continue to think of the way things used to be

This ache keeps coming and coming back to me
Of the love I had for you and the love you had for me

I must continue to face day after day in this new year
Where all that remains are these aches and tears

There is no you and me
The way it used to be

I walk around and around in our home all alone
Wishing you were back here with me in our home

I just want to wrap my arms around you
And hug you the way we used to do

But once again that can only be
In my dreams of you and me

So now I must return to our bed
With all these thoughts of you and me in my head

Thinking of you and me
And the way things used to be

My pillow is wet with tears
When I think of the love we had all those years

Oh, what a wonderful day I will find
When I can leave all those aches and tears behind

When I can once again be
With my sweet Jesse for all eternity

March 18, 2023, at 8:30 a.m.

Everything All Around Me Reminds Me of My Sweet Jesse

Everything all around me reminds me of my sweet Jesse
Like the pictures, I see of Jesse and me

His clothes on the hangar on the door
Remind me of my sweet Jesse more and more

Where can I go without memories of you
And how we loved our life as two

God keeps giving me poems about me and you
And all the things we used to do

I guess it is God's way
To help me pass the day

But it is just so hard to get through the day
With my sweet dear Jesse so far away

When I look at pictures of him
Memories keep flowing in

My life was complete when he was here with me
So it is hard to accept that life will never be

So then I think of what I will do
Do I have to have breakfast, lunch, and dinner without you

My appetite is not the way it used to be
When we would eat together just you and me

It is so hard to come home and open the door
And you are not there to greet me anymore

Friends come and call to comfort me
But I just want my life back to the way it used to be

It is still so hard to face another day
When my sweet Jesse is so far away

So now all I can think of every day
When will Jesus take me far away

To once again join with my sweet Jesse
To live with him in heaven for all eternity

March 20, 2023, 3:30 a.m.

Dementia Memories of You
and Me and More

Once again, God woke me up in the middle of the night
And brought back the memories of confusion and fright

This is the story of when dementia walks in the door
And the husband that you loved is not there anymore

He had emotions he had no control of
As we tried to hang on to our love

His personality changed
And our life was rearranged

I think back again to how frightening and confusing that must have
    been
For you, my sweet husband, Jesse, and my friend

To wake up in the morning and face another day
And more confusion in your mind was on the way

You would wake up angry, frightened, and confused and walk out
    the door
Because the lady you lived with and loved was a stranger to you and
    not your wife anymore

And then that stranger walked out the door and followed you
And you were confused and didn't know what to do

You would continue to walk out the door when it was dark
To once again escape from our home in the park

You walked all the way up to the gate
And it was very late

You were in danger standing there at the gate by the door
Where cars were passing through the gate more and more

I tried to encourage you to come home with me, and you refused,
        and I didn't know what to do
So I had to make the decision to call 911 to come and take you

They took you to emergency
Where you didn't want to be

The next day I went to emergency
To take you back home with me

But you still had a lot of anger in you
And again I didn't know what to do

So again I had to make the decision that it was safer for you and me
If I just left you there in emergency and that was so hard for me.

Then you called out my name in the emergency room, "Nina, Nina"
        in a plea
As once again you were in a place that you didn't want to be as you
        wanted to go home with me

But I had to leave you there another time
For your safety and mine

All these memories come into my mind
Where peace we could not find

They finally transferred you from emergency to a room in the hos-
        pital for care
When I would go to visit you day after day while you were there

Your children, my children, grandchildren, and great-grandchildren
    visited you there
While you were under hospital care

Shortly after I placed you in hospital care
You were placed in God's care

You were then transferred to another hospital for hospice care
Where my daughter Laurie, my granddaughter, Heather, and I vis-
    ited you there

You looked so peaceful in hospice in your bed
Laying on your side with a pillow under your head

You finally left all the anger and confusion behind
Where once again God's peace you would find

All the tubes and IVs were gone
Where once you had depended upon

You always loved to hear me sing to you
So I brought my CD for the nurses to play for you

Our forty-fifth wedding anniversary was October 7, 2022
So I decided to write a love letter to you

I read that love letter to you while you lay in hospice so peacefully
    in your bed
With a pillow so comfortably placed under your head

Before I read that love letter to you
I had the nurse remove your oxygen mask so I could kiss you

They said you may not respond, but you knew I was there
So I kissed you, and you kissed me, so I knew you loved me and you
    cared

There was no more anger and confusion there
Because you continued to be in God's peace and care

So once again I sat by your bed
Where you lay peacefully with the pillow under your head

I read my love letter to you
That I wrote on October 7, 2022

I wrote this letter on our forty-fifth anniversary
About the love I had for you and the love you had for me

The memories come pouring in when you were transferred to hos-
    pice on Monday, October 17, 2022, at 10 p.m.
And God's love took your breath away on October 19, 2022, at 7:10
    p.m. to bring you peace once again

God helped me plan a beautiful, joyful "Celebration of Life" service
    for you on November 19, 2022
And all your family and mine and old friends and new came to that
    special service just for you

Then on November 26, 2022, God gave me poems to write about
    the love I have for you
They are words of love and memories of the love you had for me and
    the love I had for you

God continued giving me poems, just a few
Once again about the love you had for me and the love I had for you

That love doesn't stop because you have passed away
Because when God thinks it is time, I plan to come to visit you
    someday

And we will be together once again, my sweet Jesse
In our home in heaven that God has planned for you and me for all
     eternity

I guess this is the time to bring this poem to an end
Because I know that God has more poems for me to write for Him
     once again

March 20, 2023, at 8:30 p.m.

As I Was Sitting in My Home Tonight, God Gave Me Another Poem to Write

As I was sitting in my home tonight
God gave me another poem to write

I received a medical bill in the mail that I have already paid for
They told me I have yet to pay this bill and more

As far as I can see
All my bills are paid by me

You can take a look
To confirm this in my checkbook

I know God is helping me
To take care of all my responsibilities

These same responsibilities
My sweet husband, Jesse, used to take care of for me

But since God took my sweet Jesse away
These bills are now my responsibility to pay

God keeps waking me up with words to share
To let me know how much He cares

Today God woke me up at 3:30 a.m.
To write another poem once again

At 5:30 a.m., I finished the poem and went back to bed
To lay down my sleepy head

At 7:30 a.m.
I woke up to feed my sweet kitty again

I went back to bed at nine thirty
As I was still so sleepy

So now it is two
And the cat is hungry, and I am too

These are the crazy hours God has given me
To share these poems for all to see since he woke me up at three thirty

All I have done since 3:30 a.m.
Is to wake up and write God's poems and go back to sleep again

It is now 6:30 p.m.
And it is time to feed my kitty again

Now I am going to look at the calendar to see
If there are awaiting any scheduled dates and responsibilities

It is now 8:30 p.m., and I have finished another poem from God to me
So I can share another poem with my family

Time marches on, and it is 9:30 p.m., and I am getting ready for bed
For I have had a busy day, and it is once again time to lay down my
    sleepy head

Who knows, God may wake me up again in the early morn
And another poem will be born.

So now this poem must come to an end
Before God wakes me up again

April 21, 2023, at 2:27 a.m.

God's Poetry for All the World to See

It's up to me to share God's poetry for all the world to see
That is why he has given these poems to me

That is why he has given me these words to rhyme
To share with others as they flow in and out of me all the time

So what am I to do
But to obey God and share God's words with you

So early in the morn, I get up and down out of bed
To write down and share with you what God has said

It is now early in the morning, and it is now two fifty-three
And more words from God are written in poetry

So now I am asking God to let me go to sleep
And save all these words to keep

To save them for another day
So that I can share with you what God has to say

So now that I have had a good night's sleep
I can once again share all of God's words to keep

I can continue to write all the words you see
From God's poetry

God, what am I going to do about these coming years
As I continue to go day after day with all these tears

I know You are helping me every step of the way
Until I can be with my sweet Jesse on that last day

These words came to me in the early morn
And another of God's poems was born

So once again, another one of God's poems must come to an end
As I share God's poems with my family and friends

So keep thinking of me and all the days that will be
Until I can spend all eternity with my sweet dear husband, Jesse

The First Day of Christmas for Me in 2022

As I was laying this evening in our bed
God put these familiar Christmas song lyrics into my head

"On the first day of Christmas, my true love gave to me
A partridge in a pear tree"

Actually, on that first day of Christmas in 2022,
My sweet Jesse, there was only me, and there was no you

There was no partridge in a pear tree
There was no you, there was only me

For God had taken you, my true love, Jesse, from me
From our home to your new home in heaven for all eternity

The days that followed in 2023
Were not what I would have chosen for me

Because, my sweet husband, Jesse, you were not at home with me
Where I prayed you would always be

Every day that goes by in this new year of 2023
It is still so quiet for me without you, my sweet Jesse

I look at pictures of you from all the passing years
And once again, my eyes are filled with tears

But every day that goes by, God is comforting me in our home
As he fills my thoughts of you with words that turn into this poem.

As God continues to give me this poem about you, my sweet Jesse,
    and me
I remember the love I had for you and the love you had for me and
    the way our life used to be

I must learn to live my new life without you, my dear sweet Jesse
As God helps me face the days ahead filled with grief and adversity

Days and days go by in 2023
As I sit here without you, my sweet Jesse

And still, all that remains are tears
And memories of all those years

So until that time, I will wait to see
How many more Christmases God has in store for me

He said He will be here with me through every passing day
While you, my dear sweet Jesse, are oh so far away

So each day, my dear Jesse, I will sit here in our home and wait
    patiently
Until Jesus will take me to be with you in our new home for all
    eternity

About the Author

The author's name is Nina Dean. She is eighty-four years old. She lives in Orlando, Florida. Her husband, Jesse James Dean Jr., passed away on October 19, 2022, at the age of ninety-five. Their forty-fifth wedding anniversary was October 7, 2022. On November 26, 2022, she began receiving words from God to comfort her as she grieved for her sweet Jesse. God has used her to turn these words into a book of fifty-seven poems  to comfort others as they have comforted her. Now in June of 2023, these poems have been submitted to Christian Faith Publishing. God also gave her the title of the book, God's Book of Poems for You and Me as We Face Grief and Adversity.

www.ingramcontent.com/pod-product-compliance
Lightning Source LLC
Chambersburg PA
CBHW020625160726
47991CB00002BA/940